Balboa Press books may be ordered through booksellers or by contacting:

Balboa Press
A Division of Hay House
1663 Liberty Drive
Bloomington, IN 47403
www.balboapress.com
1 (877) 407-4847

Because of the dynamic nature of the Internet, any web addresses or links contained
in this book may have changed since publication and may no longer be valid. The views
expressed in this work are solely those of the author and do not necessarily reflect the
views of the publisher, and the publisher hereby disclaims any responsibility for them.

The author of this book does not dispense medical advice or prescribe the use of any
technique as a form of treatment for physical, emotional, or medical problems without the
advice of a physician, either directly or indirectly. The intent of the author is only to offer
information of a general nature to help you in your quest for emotional and spiritual well-
being. In the event you use any of the information in this book for yourself, which is your
constitutional right, the author and the publisher assume no responsibility for your actions.

Any people depicted in stock imagery provided by Thinkstock are models,
and such images are being used for illustrative purposes only.
Certain stock imagery © Thinkstock.

ISBN: 978-1-5043-4721-1 (sc)
ISBN: 978-1-5043-4783-9 (e)

Print information available on the last page.

Balboa Press rev. date: 09/02/2016

Only Four Years Old

by Syeena Malone

BALBOA.
PRESS

A DIVISION OF HAY HOUSE

Elizabeth
Isn't Afraid To Ride Anymore

Linda Williams Allen

authorHOUSE®

AuthorHouse™
1663 Liberty Drive
Bloomington, IN 47403
www.authorhouse.com
Phone: 1 (800) 839-8640

Published by AuthorHouse   10/14/2015

ISBN: 978-1-5049-0000-3 (sc)
ISBN: 978-1-4969-7499-0 (e)

Print information available on the last page.

This book is printed on acid-free paper.

DEDICATION

In loving memory of my mother, Elizabeth
Joyce Williams. She believed in me.

This book is dedicated to my grandchildren: Alexia,
Asya, Alissia, Caleb, Kailyn, Makenzi and Aiden;
my great granddaughter, Brooklynn; and my great
nieces: Aiyana, Makenna, Meelah, and Aliviah Faye.

Although this is a true story (written several years
ago) about Alexia overcoming her fear of riding the
meanest-looking roller coaster ever, it is fun reading
for all of you to enjoy! When you are fearful, remember
that things may not be as scary as they seem.
Granna/Aunt Faye loves you ALL very very much!

Family is everything! Thank you Joseph, my
husband; Antonio and Shauna, my son and
daughter; and their spouses—with all my love!

A very special honor and appreciation to my best friend, Gale M. Wilkins. For over 30 years, you have been real. I love you Gale!

Heartfelt thanks and love goes to all of my family: especially my dad, Herbert Williams, and my wonderful DC Metro and North Carolina friends. I am grateful for all of you.

Elizabeth
Isn't Afraid To Ride Anymore

When Elizabeth was a little girl, she regularly visited her grandparents who live near Washington, DC.

They often went to a fun

place called Jeepers.

Jeepers is an indoor,

family entertainment park.

Elizabeth plays lots of games because she can win tickets, which are redeemed for neat gifts and toys.

She always rode the
Tilt-A-Whirl before eating just
in case she got a little dizzy.

The food was delicious. Her favorites were the cotton candy and corn dogs. She was fascinated with the look and feel of the cotton candy. The hardest part was choosing a flavor.

Two of Elizabeth's favorites

are the bumper cars

and the airplane.

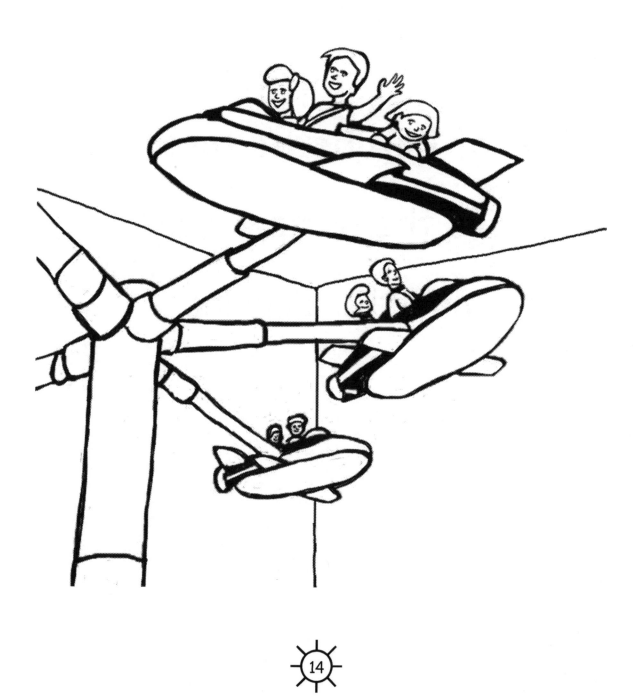

She just cannot go to Jeepers

without riding them. In fact,

she loves them so much she

usually rides them many times.

She loves spinning around
and bumping the other kids.

Sometimes she gets to bump

mommies and daddies.

That really makes her

feel like a big girl.

Another one of her favorites

is the soft play area.

The goal is to get to the
long, bumpy slides.

This is a huge maze with
winding tunnel slides
and nets that allow kids
to climb in and out.

She screams to the top of her lungs all the way down and then goes back for more.

There are five slides, and it's really cool when she and other kids all go down screaming together.

There is one ride that Elizabeth absolutely refused to get on. It is called the Python Pit.

This is a green roller coaster

that looks like a python.

It also goes really fast.

It even goes through a dark cave area. It's not haunted or extremely frightening—just a little too dark for Elizabeth.

Her grandparents always tried

to talk her into riding it, but

she absolutely would not!

One day—much to everyone's surprise—Elizabeth said to her grandfather, "If you will ride with me today, I will ride the Python."

Of course everyone thought that she would chicken out. However, she reluctantly got on; but she held on very tight to her grandfather.

As her grandmother, Granna, looked on, she could see that Elizabeth was very afraid and had begun to cry.

When the ride went into the first pit, she let out a very loud scream; but by the end of the ride she was laughing.

Elizabeth now realizes that the ride wasn't as fast as it looked, and she was very proud of herself.

She even said that she
wanted to ride it again
one day. Needless to say:
"one day" meant "another
day." She was pooped.

Elizabeth was so tired, she decided to save the Skee-ball game for next time.

The last thing was to redeem her tickets. Granna helped her feed the tickets into the ticket-eating machine, and the total count was 431.

Elizabeth chose a pink, heart-shaped jewelry box with a lock; but she needed 1000 tickets for it.

Rather than using her tickets on just anything, she decided to save them until she had enough for the jewelry box and other gifts.

That was a very good decision.

She thanked her grandparents,

and they all headed home.

When they got home, Elizabeth put her coupons—which were proof of the 431 tickets she had won—in a very safe place.

She will add them to what she wins next time and redeem them for large prizes.

Elizabeth was so tired,

she had to take a nap.

ABOUT THE ILLUSTRATOR

Elysia "Lisa" Netter was born in Ohio in 1995. She has been drawing since early childhood and has always loved art. Elysia is a self-employed artist who specializes in drawing portraits and characters. She currently lives in North Carolina, where she is attending college for Art and Design. Elysia enjoys video games and comic books. She hopes to one day be a video game character artist, where she can bring her art to life.